NONET: a 9-line poem. The first line has 9 syllables. Each line subtracts a syllable until the ninth line has 1 syllable. Nonets can also "grow" from 1 syllable to 9.

sycamore

cedar

QUATRAIN: a 4-line poem or 4-line stanza in a longer poem.

MATH: a poem that describes its subject using math concepts.

PERSONA: a poem written from the point of view of the poem's subject.

aspen

SEDOKA: an unrhymed Japanese poetry form with 2 stanzas of 3 lines each. The stanzas follow a 5-7-7 syllable count.

TWO-VOICE: a poem written from two different points of view. It is meant to be read by two speakers.

ZENO: a poetry form invented by former Children's Poet Laureate J. Patrick Lewis. A zeno consists of 10 lines of verse with the syllable count 8-4-2-1, 4-2-1, 4-2-1. Lines 4, 7, and 10 rhyme.

banyan

To Gabby, Emilee, and Karlee,
beautiful branches on our family tree

—MICHELLE

For my nephew, A.J.

—ANNE

SLEEPING BEAR PRESS™

2395 South Huron Parkway, Suite 200, Ann Arbor, MI 48104
www.sleepingbearpress.com © Sleeping Bear Press

Printed and bound in the United States.
10 9 8 7 6 5 4 3 2 1

Library of Congress Cataloging-in-Publication Data
Names: Schaub, Michelle, author. | Lambelet, Anne, illustrator.
Title: Leafy landmarks : travels with trees / by Michelle Schaub ;
  illustrated by Anne Lambelet.
Description: Ann Arbor, MI : Sleeping Bear Press, [2024] | Audience: Ages
  6-10. | Summary: "Through a variety of poetic forms, readers journey
  across the continental United States to visit 14 historic tree sites.
  Trees include the Emancipation Oak in Virginia to the Methuselah tree in
  California. Facts cover geography, history, and nature"-- Provided by publisher.
Identifiers: LCCN 2023033959 | ISBN 9781534112872 (hardcover)
Subjects: LCSH: Historic trees--United States--Juvenile literature. |
  Trees--United States--Juvenile literature. | Historic sites--United
  States--Juvenile literature.
Classification: LCC SD383.3.U6 S33 2024 | DDC 582.160973--dc23/eng/20231031
LC record available at https://lccn.loc.gov/2023033959

LEAFY LANDMARKS

Travels with Trees

By **Michelle Schaub** *and illustrated by* **Anne Lambelet**

PUBLISHED *by* SLEEPING BEAR PRESS™

HIT THE ROAD
(POETRY FORM: QUATRAIN)

Come take an arbor road trip
in search of sights TREE-mendous;
landmarks of the timber kind,
with stories quite stupendous.

We'll seek out trees superlative
in height and size and age;
others famous for their role
on history's grand stage.

We'll zigzag up steep mountainsides,
meander shore to shore,
and learn about these trees through verse.
Branch out, and let's explore!

United States of America
State Boundary

300 KM
0
300 Miles

The Wishing Tree

Grove of Titans

Methuselah

Pando Aspen Grove

General Sherman

petrified forest

SHADY HAVEN

poetry form: nonet

With limbs spread wide in invitation,
this tree became a safe haven.
Men and women, boys and girls
flocked to its dappled shade.
Beneath breeze-kissed leaves
they learned to read.
Slaves no more.
Hopeful.
Free.

Location: Hampton University, Hampton, Virginia
Species: Live Oak

After the American Civil War erupted in 1861, hundreds of enslaved African Americans escaped to Fort Monroe, a Union stronghold in Confederate Virginia. Previously, Virginia law prohibited slaves from receiving an education. Mary Peake, a free Black woman, began teaching the runaways to read and write. She held her first classes beneath an oak tree. Although Mary died in 1862, her dream to educate her people continued. In January 1863, President Abraham Lincoln issued his Emancipation Proclamation. The Black community gathered around the oak to hear a reading of this proclamation. It declared the freedom of all slaves held in Confederate territories. After the war ended, a college was founded near the tree to educate Black students. The Emancipation Oak still stands on the campus of Hampton University as a reminder that all people deserve the freedom to learn.

EMANCIPATION OAK

Gracious Gift

poetry form:

sedoka

spring arrives, defies
the bleakness of winter skies
with pink confetti showers

bursting petals swirl
here and far across the sea
a friendship celebration

Japanese Cherry Blossom Trees

Location: Washington, D.C.

Species: Ornamental Cherry Tree

A sure sign of spring in Washington, D.C., is the blooming of thousands of cherry blossom trees. People treasure the flowers, while birds enjoy their small bitter fruit. In 1912, the city of Tokyo presented a gift of more than 3,000 Japanese cherry blossom trees to the city of Washington as a symbol of friendship between the United States and Japan. First Lady Helen Herron Taft and Viscountess Chinda, the wife of the Japanese ambassador, planted the first two trees in Potomac Park. Since then, several first ladies, including Hillary Clinton and Michelle Obama, have continued that tradition by planting new cherry blossom trees in D.C. parks in the spring. Today, the National Cherry Blossom Festival welcomes more than a million visitors to the capital city each year.

Boston Liberty Tree

COMMONWEAL[T]

Location: Boston, Massachusetts
Species: Elm

At the corner of Washington and Essex Streets in downtown Boston, a plaque marks the spot where a stately elm once grew. On August 14, 1765, when Britain controlled the American colonies, angry colonists gathered beneath this elm. They were furious with the British for passing the Stamp Act, which taxed newspapers and official documents. In protest, they hung a straw-stuffed figure of a tax collector from the tree's limbs. These protestors became known as the Sons of Liberty. Their tree was the first Liberty Tree. Soon, Sons of Liberty groups formed in many colonial towns. Each group chose its own tree as a rallying place. To the British, these trees symbolized the colonists' disobedience. In 1775, British soldiers chopped down the Boston Liberty Tree. The British destroyed other Liberty Trees during the Revolutionary War, but they could not uproot the colonists' will to be free.

SONS of LIBERTY 1766
INDEPENDENCE of their COUNTRY
1776

OF MASSACHUSETTS

Leaves of Change...

poetry form: cherita

Restless, daring, surreptitious.

Held against
the British wishes.

Rebels seeking liberty
met beneath the boughs of trees
and spread dissent like windswept leaves.

SEEDS OF A NATION

poetry form: apostrophe

Star-spangled arbor.
Patriot true.
Does the sap in your branches
run red, white, and blue?
Each ring of your trunk
shares a year with our nation.
Both grown from seeds sown
with *the* Declaration.

TREE OF

Location: Portsmouth, New Hampshire

Species: Horse Chestnut

1776: the birth year of the United States and a special horse chestnut tree. The tree was planted from seeds Founding Father William Whipple gathered on a historic visit to Philadelphia.

At the time, revolution seethed through the American colonies. Colonists wanted to make an official break from Britain. Whipple was one of 56 delegates of the Continental Congress, a government put in place by the colonists. The

INDEPENDENCE

delegates traveled to Philadelphia, the center of Revolutionary government, to sign the Declaration of Independence. This document proclaimed the colonies to be free and independent. While in Philadelphia, Whipple gathered some prickly horse chestnut seeds as a reminder of his journey. When he returned to New Hampshire, Whipple likely had his enslaved servant, Prince Whipple, who had also traveled to Philadelphia with William, plant these seeds outside his home. Today, both that tree and the nation still stand strong.

ARBOR~NAUTS

poetry form: narrative

MOON TREE

Location: Camp Koch, Cannelton, Indiana (Other moon trees exist at various US sites.)

Species: Sycamore (Other moon trees include sweetgum, redwood, and Douglas fir.)

If it weren't for teacher Joan Goble, Moon Trees might have been forgotten. In 1996, Joan and her students were curious about a Girl Scout camp tree that bore the label "Moon Tree." They contacted NASA and Apollo missions expert Dr. David Williams. Dr. Williams did not know the tree's story, but he was determined to find out. Through research, Dr. Williams discovered that the tree, as a seed, had rocketed to the moon aboard Apollo 14. On January 31, 1971, astronaut Stuart Roosa had carried tree seeds in his personal pack at the request of NASA and the US Forest Service. They wanted to test the effect of space travel on the seeds' growth.* When the mission returned to Earth, the "Moon Trees" were planted around the country, but the location of many was not recorded. After learning about the Camp Koch tree, Dr. Williams created a list of all known Moon Trees. Learn more on the NASA website.

*To date, scientists have not noted any differences between Moon Trees and their earthbound relatives.

Trees are steadfast, rooted things,
anchored in one place.
Launching tree seeds to the moon?
Arbor-nauts in space?
Preposterous.
OUT-LAND-ish.

But NASA was intrigued
to learn how space affects seeds' growth.
The astronauts agreed.
So tree seeds by the hundreds
joined Apollo 14's crew.
Lift off.

Orbit.
Back to Earth.

A lunar trek debut.
Then the seeds were planted,
and they grew . . .
and grew . . .
and grew.
Now they stretch limbs skyward,

where, as seeds, they soared moon-bound,
saluting exploration

from firm stations
on the ground.

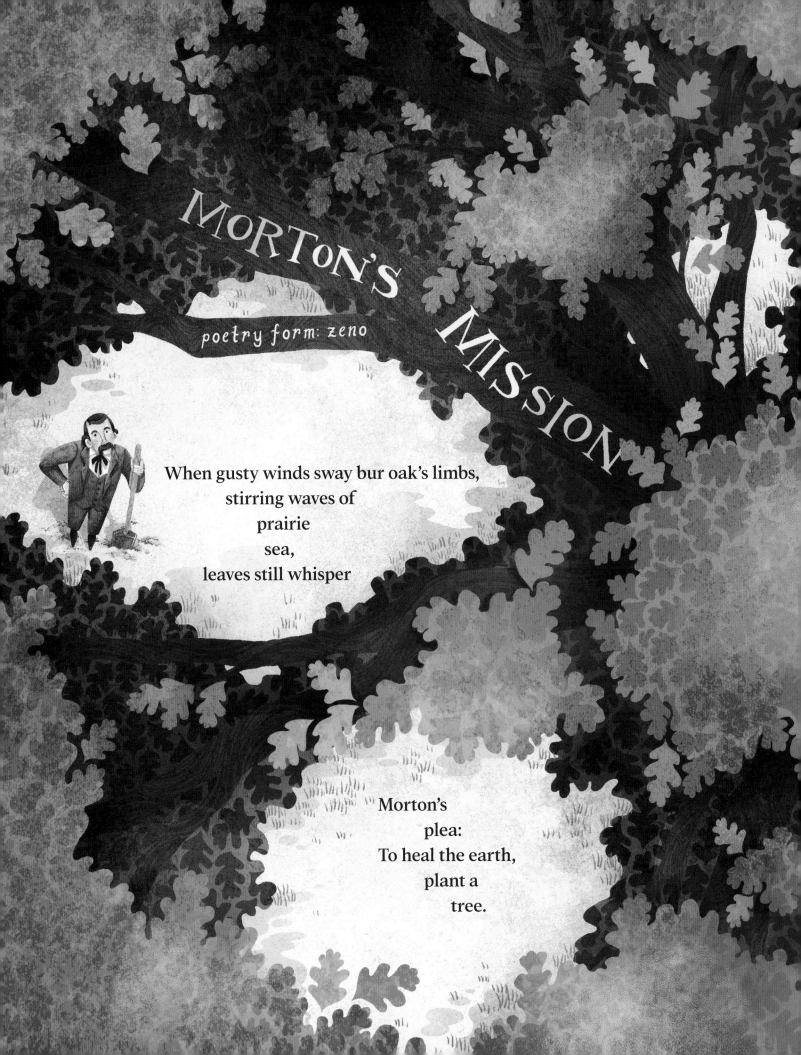

MORTON'S MISSION

poetry form: zeno

When gusty winds sway bur oak's limbs,
stirring waves of
prairie
sea,
leaves still whisper

Morton's
plea:
To heal the earth,
plant a
tree.

Location: Arbor Day Farm, Nebraska City, Nebraska

Species: Bur Oak

J. Sterling Morton arrived in Nebraska City, Nebraska, in 1855, and built a home on a hillside outside of town.

ARBOR DAY OAK

From this spot, Morton could peer across his land to where a bur oak grew. A few scattered trees, like the oak, thrived on the plains. Yet as more settlers arrived, they chopped down trees for houses and fuel. The state of Nebraska became known as a treeless desert. Morton set out to challenge that notion. He wrote newspaper articles rallying people to "plant trees." Then Morton had a great idea. Why not set aside one day each year as a tree-planting holiday? He proposed the idea to the state board of agriculture, and it was approved. April 10, 1872, became the first Arbor Day. Today, Arbor Day is celebrated around the world. The bur oak still grows on Morton's estate, now called Arbor Day Farm, where volunteers continue to spread the message to "plant trees."

ONE-TREE FOREST

poetry form: etheree

One
small seed,
dressed in fleece,
dances downwind,
settles near a lake,
feels Earth's warm hug, awakes,
periscopes a lone, pale stem,
matures through time, weaves roots, extends,
sprouts a legion of breeze-quaking trees.
A pearly forest, spread from one small seed.

PANDO ASPEN GROVE

Location: Fishlake National Forest, Utah

Species: Aspen

Pando means "I spread" in Latin. A fitting name for a grove of aspens that stretches more than 106 acres in Utah, the size of 90 football fields. Above the ground, this vast grove looks like thousands of individual trees, but it is actually one organism. Below the ground, a single root system spreads and sends up new trunks. The trunks are all clones, meaning each is an exact genetic copy of the others. Weighing more than 13 million pounds, with more than 40,000 trunks, Pando is one of the largest known still-living organisms on Earth. It is also one of the oldest. Scientists believe Pando sprouted from a single seed around the end of the last ice age.

Wishes...

poetry form: list

. . . for sunshine,
clean oceans, soft rain,
a world free of homelessness,
bullies, and pain.
For unicorns, puppies,
and warm meals for all,
fairness and justice,
a new soccer ball.
For skateboards
and kindness
and pizza on trees,
a land without weapons,
a cure for disease.
For best friends to stay close
and not move away.

For laughter and dancing
to fill up each day.
For bravery, patience,
wisdom, and grace.
A forest of wishes
takes root
in this place.

THE WISHING TREE

Thousands of paper cards tied with colorful ribbon hang from an old cedar tree in the Capitol Hill neighborhood of Seattle. Each strip contains a wish made by a passerby. Some wishes are whimsical, some serious, but they all flutter in the breeze with hopeful spirit. This particular "wishing tree" was started in 2014 by property owner Jane Hamel, but the concept is centuries old and is practiced in several cultures around the world. The Seattle Wishing Tree has brought the community together. One neighbor donated a laminating machine to protect wishes from soggy weather. Another added a bench for wish-makers to sit on. Others volunteer by tying wishes to the tree. As the sign propped up against the tree explains, *Something magical happens when we all wish in the same place.*

LOFTY TITANS

poetry form: concrete

Crowns
in
the
clouds,
these
lofty
Titans
tower
above
their
arbor
friends.
Some
taller
than
Lady
Liberty,
they
extend

Grove of Titans

Location: Redwood National and State Parks, California

Species: Coast Redwood

Coast redwoods, the tallest trees on Earth, loom like lofty giants. Historically, they grew along the coast from Big Sur, California, to southern Oregon. Today, only about five percent remain due to a century of heavy logging. Conservation efforts from local Indigenous tribes, gardening groups, non-profit organizations, government agencies, and countless individuals saved these remarkable trees.

over
300
feet
from
knobby
toes
to
leafy
heads.
Good
thing
they
never
have
to
stoop
to
unknot
tangled
shoelace
roots.

Redwood forests not only provide homes for hundreds of other plant and animal species, they clean the air we breathe more than any other tree. They also play an integral role in many Indigenous cultures. While there are several northern California locations to see coast redwoods, the Grove of Titans is one of the best. You'll see many trees towering more than 300 feet, including several that challenge as the world's tallest tree!

GENERAL SHERMAN
MEASURES UP
poetry form: math poem

Ten blue whales upon a scale
would match its massive weight.

To reach its height in stacked giraffes,
you'd add up eight plus eight.

Three rhinos lined up tail to horn
would fit across its base.

A ring of thirteen silverbacks
could form a tree embrace.

When taken all together,
these stats from height to girth,

it's clear to see—
just why this tree's
the *biggest* one on Earth.

GENERAL SHERMAN

Location: Sequoia National Park, California
Species: Giant Sequoia

Other trees stake their claim as the tallest, oldest, and widest. But the giant sequoia known as General Sherman has the largest volume of wood, making it the biggest. Check out this tree's massive stats:

Height: 275 feet
Diameter: 36.5 feet (at its base)
Circumference at ground: 102.6 feet
Overall volume: 52,500 cubic feet

The tree is named after William Tecumseh Sherman, a general in the Union Army during the American Civil War. From 1890–1916, Sequoia National Park was patrolled by the military, which is why some of the biggest sequoias are named after military men. Today, the top of the General Sherman tree is dead, so its trunk does not get taller. However, the tree continues to grow wider, increasing its mammoth volume each year.

Advice from an Ancient

poetry form: epistle

Dear Sprout,

Take a look about.
Life is no pruned arbor here.
This arid, barren mountainside
will toughen up your tender hide.
Wind and ice don't play nice.
You'll be mangled, tangled, tattered,
bent and battered.
You'll grow haggard, but resistant.
And if you are persistent,
in a thousand years or so
you'll come to be
a wizened, wise survivor
just like me.

Sincerely,
Old Bristlecone

Methuselah

Location: Schulman Grove, Inyo National Forest, California
Species: Bristlecone Pine

Bristlecone pines are the oldest living single trees on Earth. The most famous of these ancients is Methuselah. It resides on a stark mountainside in California. Methuselah was discovered in 1957 by Edmund Schulman, a scientist looking for long-lived trees to help with his research on past climates. Schulman used a special tool to remove wood from Methuselah's trunk to count the tree's rings. He knew that bristlecone pines could live for thousands of years. They survive because most of their body is dead wood that is resistant to fires and insects. Bristlecones also save energy by growing slowly, adding less than an inch to their waistline in a century. When Schulman counted this bristlecone's rings, he was shocked. It had more than 4,600, which made Methuselah the oldest known living tree on Earth. Perhaps even older bristlecones cling to the mountainside, yet to be discovered.

Triassic Timber
poetry form: persona

As trees, we were giants,
strong and defiant,
skyscrapers bold and green.
We loomed along rivers,
spurning Earth's shivers,
unfazed by the ancient scene.

Though jagged-toothed beasts
hunting for feasts
menaced the land as they fed,
and snappy-jawed swimmers
made the seas simmer,
we basked in the sun without dread.

Sure, the land rocked,
and our limbs felt the shock.
We swayed,
but we stayed dignified.

Then tragedy struck.
We were buried in muck,
and time left us

PETRIFIED.

PETRIFIED FOREST

Location: Petrified Forest National Park, Arizona
Species: Ancient Conifers, Ginkgoes, and Cycads

Arizona's petrified forest doesn't look like a forest. Instead of living trees, piles
of rainbow-colored logs litter the grassland. More than 200 million years ago,
during the Triassic Period, these logs were towering trees that grew along rivers.
The trees shared their habitat with fearsome creatures, like Postosuchus, one of
the top land predators, and Smilosuchus, a long-snouted aquatic reptile. During
most of the Triassic Period, Earth's tectonic plates were stuck together like puzzle
pieces. But then the land began to break apart, ending the Triassic Period with a
rise in volcanic activity. Over time, rivers dried out and trees tumbled. The fallen
trees were buried under layers of sediment, material that settled over time.
As the wood decomposed, water carried minerals such as quartz, iron,
and carbon into the wood. This "petrified" the trees, turning them into
colorful stone relics.

S·u·r·v·i·v·o·r T·r·e·e

Species: Elm

Location: Oklahoma City, Oklahoma

A bomb exploded in front of the Alfred P. Murrah Federal Building in Oklahoma City on April 19, 1995. The blast killed 168 people and destroyed or damaged more than 300 surrounding buildings. At the time, it was the worst act of terrorism to take place on US soil. As the dust settled, a lone elm stood amid the destruction, battered and blackened, but alive. When a memorial was planned, community members insisted on including this elm. Today the Survivor Tree grows as a focal point of the Oklahoma City National Memorial, reminding visitors of the strength of the human spirit to withstand tragedy. After the attack on the World Trade Center in 2001, the mayor of New York City received a special gift from the mayor of Oklahoma City: a Survivor Tree seedling. Survivor Tree seedlings are distributed each year, spreading the message of hope and healing far beyond Oklahoma City.

H·o·p·e S·u·r·v·i·v·e·s

poetry form: contrast

Hate
rumbles.
Tumbles towers.
Crumbles concrete
into rubble.
Triggers trouble.

But . . .

Hope
clings.
Digs in roots.
Springs forth shoots.
Sings in green
unfurling leaves.

Survives
and
thrives.

RESOURCEFUL ROOTS:
A TWO-VOICE SALUTE
poetry form: two-voice

Edison: inventor.

Banyan: "walking" tree.

**Both made their mark
by acting**
innovatively.

Edison
asked questions.
He thought outside the box.

*Banyan grows
aboveground roots.
Its shape's unorthodox.*

His patents led to progress.
His ideas still pervade.

*Its root limbs form
a labyrinth,
providing boundless shade.*

Vast, adaptive banyan.

Creative engineer.

**Both show us how
to flourish**
i f w e s t r e t c h
and persevere.

THE BANYAN TREE

Location: Edison & Ford Winter Estates, Fort Myers, Florida
Species: Banyan

A tangle of trunks sprawls across the garden of Thomas Edison's Florida estate. This tangle is a single tree. The "trunks" are fully formed aerial roots. Banyans sprout roots in an unusual way: from their upper branches. These roots snake downward, forming pillar trunks. The banyan is often called the "Walking Tree" because those roots develop into a support system for new branches as the tree grows outward. Edison planted the banyan in his experimental garden. He was searching for a plant source for rubber that could be grown in the United States. (After testing thousands of plants, Edison found goldenrod, a perennial herb with yellow buds, to be the most suitable rubber source.) When Edison planted the banyan, it was around four feet high, with a two-inch trunk. Over time, both the banyan and Edison's ideas spread. In his lifetime, Edison received 1,093 US patents for his inventions. Today, the Edison Banyan is considered one of the biggest banyan trees in the continental United States.

MY LANDMARK TREE
(poetry form: quatrain)

Don't need to travel very far
to find my favorite tree.
It stands outside my window
and watches over me.

When I was just a little twig,
I toddled in its shade.
And as I sprout, no matter if
I'm cheerful, sad, afraid . . .

my tree is there to lean upon,
read under, climb carefree.
I love my tree *TREE*-mendously—
it shares *my* history.

Be a Tree Champion

Thick forests once covered much of North America. The trees in those forests were considered an endless resource. Today more than 90 percent of America's original forests have been cleared away. When trees are designated as landmarks, it helps people understand the role of trees in communities. Not only do trees clean the air and improve the view, but they hold important stories deep in their roots. People like J. Sterling Morton recognized the value of trees and made efforts to protect existing trees and plant new ones.

You can be a tree champion too!

Take a Tree Road Trip

The trees in this collection are only a sampling of hundreds of landmark trees you can find around the country. Want to discover a monumental tree close to home? Most states have a list of local historic trees. You can look up these lists online. Want to track down really big trees? American Forests, a citizens' conservation organization, keeps a National Register of Champion Trees. You can find this list of super-sized trees on the American Forests website.

When visiting historic trees, remember to be respectful. Admire them from designated paths or viewing areas. If too many visitors walk on the soil around a tree, it can harm the tree's root system. Take pictures, but leave the tree's leaves, needles, and seeds as part of the natural ecosystem.

Plant Your Own Landmark

You don't have to wait for Arbor Day to celebrate trees. Planting a tree is a wonderful way to mark an important moment. You can plant a sapling for someone's birthday or anniversary or to remember a special person. You might plant a tree in your yard, or you could make a donation to have a tree planted in an arboretum or a public place. The Arbor Day Foundation even has a program where you can plant trees in national forests in honor of a special person or pet. Visit the Arbor Day Foundation website to learn more. The trees you plant today will become part of *your* history.

Acknowledgments

A forest of gratitude to the following individuals and organizations for their expert input:

The Hampton University Museum; Ann McClellan, author of *The Cherry Blossom Festival*; Stephanie Hewson and Jeff Barraclough, Moffatt-Ladd House & Garden; Joan Goble; Dr. David Williams, Planetary Scientist, NASA; Arbor Day Farm; Mike Elson, Fishlake National Forest Supervisor; Terry Holsclaw, Fishlake National Forest Silviculturist; Kurt Robins, Fremont River District Ranger; Cody Clark, Fremont River District Recreation Program Manager; Naomi Gordon, Fishlake National Forest Public Affairs Officer; Jane Hamel; Patrick Taylor, Interpretation and Education Program Manager, Redwoods National and State Parks; Rebecca Paterson, Public Affairs Specialist, Sequoia and Kings Canyon National Parks; Rebecca Hutto, District Recreation Officer, Inyo National Forest; Dr. Adam Marsh, Lead Paleontologist, National Park Service; Hallie Larsen, Interpretive Ranger, National Park Service; Dr. William Parker, Resources Program Manager, National Park Service; the Oklahoma City National Memorial & Museum; Matthew Andres, Curatorial Registrar, Edison & Ford Winter Estates

live oak

COAST redwood

CONTRAST: a poem that shows the contrast between two people, places, things, or ideas.

APOSTROPHE: a poem in which the narrator speaks directly to a person, place, idea, or thing.

bur oak

CHERITA: a poem of 3 stanzas that tells a story. The first stanza has 1 line, the second has 2 lines, and the third stanza has 3 lines.

CONCRETE: a poem that is arranged on the page to take the shape of the poem's subject.

EPISTLE: a letter in verse.

elm

ETHEREE: a 10-line poem. The first line has 1 syllable. Each line adds a syllable until the tenth line has 10 syllables. Etherees can also "shrink" from 10 syllables to 1.

bristlecone pine

LIST: presents a list of items, people, places, or ideas.

horse chestnut

NARRATIVE: a poem that tells a story.

giant sequoia